D1011548

# Relationships

## What
## It Takes
## to Be
## a Friend

### Pamela Reeve

Multnomah Books—Sisters, Oregon

**Relationships, What It Takes to Be a Friend**
published by Multnomah Books
*a part of the Questar publishing family*

© 1997 by Pamela Reeve

*International Standard Book Number: 1-57673-044-1*
Design and illustrations by Nina Chrysanthou
Edited by Larry Libby
Printed in Mexico

Most Scripture quotations are from the *New International Version*
© 1973, 1984 by International Bible Society
used by permission of Zondervan Publishing House

Also quoted:

The *New American Standard Bible (NASB)*
© 1960, 1977 by the Lockman Foundation; used by permission

For information:
QUESTAR PUBLISHERS, INC.
POST OFFICE BOX 1720
SISTERS, OREGON 97759

Library of Congress Cataloging-in-Publication Data:

97   98   99   00   01   —   10   9   8   7   6   5   4   3   2   1

To Joyce
*Friend for the Journey*
whose strong support, encouragement and assistance
has cheered me on
for over thirty years on the path to glory.

# Contents

# *Introduction*

Networking, the Internet—these are hallmark words of our times. They present a satisfying picture of being linked up and locked in with others. In contemporary Christendom, we talk about "fellowship groups" and "shepherding groups." Again, these are words with drawing power. Yet in spite of these familiar terms on every side today, the silent cry of so many hearts is, "I'm so lonely."

Often, that dull ache barely reaches our awareness. At other times it is a pain so acute that we feel overwhelmed. No matter our age or gender or even marital status, we all have one thing in common—loneliness of heart. The cry is for deep, richly satisfying friendships.

This desire is woven into the fabric of our being. We have been created in the image of God, and the very essence of God is a Trinity united in a love relationship. Christ died to bring us back into deep relationship with God and relationship with one another. Yet how often do those human relationships fall short of our longings? The fact is, we are deeply relational beings subsisting on a starvation diet of shallow relationships. We are members of "The Lonely Crowd," as someone once termed it. We long for a few people who understand us, who genuinely care for us, people to whom we can trust our hearts and with whom we can form deep emotional bonds. In short, we want at least a few souls on this planet to whom we really matter!

How do we make friendships in the first place? Most of us expect them to "just happen"—the way they did when we were small kids. But rarely does this occur in adulthood. Some of us think our problem lies in the fact that we are not "people persons"—another of today's pet phrases. Yet I know of many who consider themselves to be eminently outgoing, who still describe their friendships as "a mile wide and an inch deep." They long for a real encounter with others.

Some of us have been burned in friendships—and aren't about to risk being hurt again. There is a great deal of truth in the message I once read on a wall poster:

*Involvement with people is always a very delicate thing…. It requires real maturity to become involved and not get all messed up.*

Often we stumble along not knowing what is wrong in our relationships or how they could be developed or improved. We believe they were meant to be more satisfying…we yearn for them to become so…but we don't know the steps to that goal. We're on an unfamiliar pathway with neither map nor landmarks.

I would like to share some thoughts about friendships—simple but fundamental truths I have gleaned over the years. As I have taught and counseled—and walked in friendships myself—these basic guidelines have proven themselves effective time after time. And they are applicable to *all* walks of life—whether you are single, married, dating, or just seeking solid friendships to enrich your life.

That's what good friendships are...enriching. And in this little book, I'd like to share some of that wealth with you.

*– Pamela Reeve*

*Two are better than one because they have a good return for their labor. For if either of them falls, the one will lift up his companion. But woe to the one who falls when there is not another to lift him up.*
Ecclesiastes 4:9-10, NASB

# God's Purpose for Relationships

Sometimes…when life seems particularly hectic and stressful…have you ever wondered why in the world you even bother with relationships?

After all…relationships can be so troubling. So inconvenient. So disappointing. So draining. So messy. So hurting.

Where else can you invest such great stores of energy with such seemingly little return? What else can raise your expectations to such absurdly high levels one moment only to dash them on the rocks the next? What other aspects of your life can be so intensely demanding of your time, your patience, your creativity, and your emotions? Do you ever want to just throw your hands up and say "Good grief! Who needs this? *Why bother?*"

You might be surprised to learn that you are in good company with such a response. Most everyone feels that way at certain troubling bends in the road along life's journey. That's why I want to take these next few pages and walk with you through a few time-tested principles of personal relationships.

As with anything of value in life, relationships take time and effort—sometimes more than we feel prepared to offer. Yet in the final accounting of things, when you really sum up life and take stock of what it's all about, relationships are the greatest treasures we will ever possess on this planet. And unlike other earthly treasures, relationships may follow us into eternity.

This world can be a dry and thirsty world. Have you noticed? Yet true friendships are bubbling springs with the capacity to meet our thirst and restore us to life—life at its best.

As such, they should be cultivated. And guarded with great care.

## It Is Not Good for Man to Be Alone…

God gives us two simple reasons for relationships in His statement regarding Adam, the prototype human being. Although the Creator's words refer specifically to husband and wife at this juncture, the basic principles apply to any kind of relationship. The LORD God said, "It is not good for the man to be alone. I will make a helper suitable for him [or, corresponding to him]" (Genesis 2:18).

The first purpose for relationship is bound up in these words: *"It's not good to be alone."* In other words, we need friendships to prevent isolation.

Why is isolation "not good"? The simple joy of companionship offers the most obvious reason. But there's an even more profound reason than that.

You and I do not grow spiritually in a relational vacuum. It is comparatively easy to relate to God when we are alone. I am never more godly—more pure, upright, loving, and patient—than when I'm all by myself...out in the mountains on an exhilarating hike...watching the quiet ripples on a sunset lake...strolling along the pounding surf leaving a single set of footprints in the sand.

If I'm totally alone, God and I have marvelous times. I find myself thinking, *God and me...this is just fine. I don't need anyone else to lean on. I don't need other people to help me grow.* And everything is mellow and tranquil until someone intrudes on my idyllic little world and begins to annoy me or frustrate me or anger me. Suddenly, all those warm, pious feelings and grand resolves I was so enjoying are put to the test.

## The Real Test

The other morning I was pondering a passage in the Book of Proverbs:

> *A fool shows his annoyance at once,*
> *but a prudent man overlooks an insult.*
> Proverbs 12:16

"Ah Lord," I said, "that *is* a piece of wisdom. That's a truth to live by. That's where I want to be, Lord. That's for me today."

Yet within two short hours, after arriving at my office, I *did not* ignore what I saw as an insult. I threw prudence out the window and showed my annoyance immediately! And all of that good spiritual input I had received and all my fine resolutions crumbled under the test.

It is in relationships, you see, that God shows me the immaturity of my faith and the corruption of my heart. It is in relationships that He demonstrates again and again, "Without Me, you can do nothing." Not even something as simple as ignoring a perceived insult.

The truth of the situation is hardly a secret. My real growth that morning did not take place as I was meditating on that Bible verse in the warm, sunny silence of my dining room. It didn't occur as I ruminated on that bit of Scripture and told the Lord, "How true, how true! Isn't that marvelous?"

The real growth came when that fine golden truth crashed into the reality of my office relationships and shattered into a thousand pieces.

Then, after blowing it and realizing I had blown it, I had to humble myself before the Lord and say, "Lord, forgive me, forgive me. Wrong way. No good. When You bring along the next test help me depend completely upon You and Your life in me to respond correctly."

In that painful, humbling moment, I grew in Christ.

We need other people—relationships. We need people to expose to us where we fall short of doing the will of God and our moment by moment need of walking in conscious fellowship with Him. Try as we might, we cannot see those defects staring into a mirror. In the presence of others, our eyes are opened to those areas within that need to grow. And as we lean on God and His life within for those areas, we experience deeper fellowship with Him…and a new dimension of joy.

Joy out of our pain. Joy out of our tears. Joy out of our humility. It is the mixed blessing brought into our lives through our relationships with others. But it is blessing indeed—through each other we come to experience God Himself. "As iron sharpens iron, so one man sharpens another" (Proverbs 27:17).

## The Other Reason…

I mentioned two reasons why God said, "It is not good to be alone."

The other reason is because *we need a "helper"*—someone suitable to provide assistance to do God's will.

When God said this about history's first human, Adam didn't need a helper to bring extra income into his household. He had all the provision he could ever want or need. He didn't need a helper to put dinner on the table. He picked it right off the trees. He didn't need a helper to mend his clothes. He didn't wear any. He didn't even need any help washing dishes. That particular chore hadn't even been invented (it must have come *after* the fall).

What then was this "helper" supposed to do? Why did Adam need an Eve?

*She was to help him to do the will of God in the world.* Together, they would exercise dominion over the earth and populate it with their children.

Proverbs adds an important warning regarding isolation.

> *An unfriendly man pursues selfish ends;*
> *he defies all sound judgment.*
> Proverbs 18:1

An unfriendly man is a selfish, short-sighted man. He is absorbed in his own interests, and sees no further than the end of his nose. The isolated person is an individualist. He says, "I can do it all myself, by my methods, and corresponding to my standards. As long as my life is right with God, everything is okay. I can do without people. In fact, people get in the way of my goals."

That sort of attitude leads to competition and self-centeredness. It is the antithesis of the helper role with its mindset of cooperation, other-centeredness, and self-giving (Ecclesiastes 4:9, 10, 12).

We *need* relationships to help each other do God's will.

When our hearts are heavy or anxious and we are struggling to accept God's will, we need someone to pray with us and for us. The true prototype human being, the Lord Jesus Christ, faced the most crushing moment of His life to that point among the gnarled olive trees of Gethsemane.

He was deeply distressed and troubled—overwhelmed with sorrow to the point of death. Yes, He knew God's will. The cross! Yet the shadow of that prospect was so heavy it literally crushed Him to the ground. What did He do in that moment of awful darkness? Yes, He prayed fervently and poured out His heart to the Father. But He also asked His three closest friends to keep watch with Him (Mark 14:33-34).

Sometimes we need another to pray for us as we battle temptation (James 5:16) or struggle in our heart to forgive someone. Sometimes we need others to pray because of the oppression of the enemy, Satan. There are times when we can't "get through" alone, and we need another with us.

At other times we need a friend to "spur us on toward love and good deeds" (Hebrews 10:24). Have you ever been contemplating something you know you ought to do (and maybe even *want* to do) but you lack the courage or boldness to take that scary first step? Sometimes all we lack is the hand of a good friend on our shoulder. Sometimes all it takes to move us into action is a smile and gentle nudge from someone who desires our best. *"Go ahead. You can do it. I'll pray for you."*

The most important time we need a friend is when we are drifting or veering off the course of God's will. We are most likely to listen to someone who has proven to be caring and trustworthy. I say most likely because often my first reaction is to be angry at my friend. It can take a while for me to feel deeply thankful for my friend's words.

This kind of faithful confrontation takes a friend who is more concerned about my highest good than in keeping a friendship she cherishes. "Faithful are the wounds of a friend" (Proverbs 27:6, NASB).

At all times we need a "helper" to do the will of God.

Through the years of my life, I have found that friends draw me "out" as well as "up." They help me discover who I am. So often I don't know what I really think—or how I really feel—until I verbalize it. Yes, introspection has its place at times and journaling is a valid personal discipline. But as Paul Tournier points out, it is in *dialogue* with others—expressing my convictions to them—that I really come to understand my true values, and what I am like at the core.

Various friends draw out various parts of my personality. Some friends accomplish that through conversation. Other quieter friends can achieve the same result through their simple, encouraging presence.

Companionship doubles the enjoyment of happy experiences—someone to share excitement with—someone to "eat and be merry with"—to celebrate with. Their presence gives an added sparkle of joy to the journey.

God's will for us is to be productive in His kingdom. Friendships forged in those shoulder-to-shoulder working environments are some of the deepest. And often a friend sharing the job doesn't simply double our creativity but quadruples it.

> *You will not find the warrior, the poet, the philosopher, or the Christian by staring in his eyes as if he were your mistress: better fight beside him, read with him, argue with him, pray with him.*
> C. S. Lewis, *The Four Loves*

God, the Designer, knew Adam's deepest need (apart from relationship with Himself)—a human relationship.

He is your Designer, too. And He knows your needs very well.

# Three Levels of Relationships

What then are relationships all about? What kinds of friendships are there? How can we make good ones? And how can we avoid the pitfalls?

Almost every relationship we will experience in life falls into one of three categories. As we begin to grasp the unique differences in these three types of relationships, we will also learn to appreciate them individually for the important roles they play in our lives. This, in turn, will help us understand what we can expect of ourselves—and others—when it comes to relationships.

## Acquaintances—*"Friends along the way"*

Most of the people in our lives fall into this first category. Along our path through life, God in His grace and kindness provides people with whom we can talk and laugh and commiserate and simply enjoy His marvelous creation. Our lives are composed of a string of individual moments, and these casual, mostly unplanned encounters add color, refreshment, and stimulating variety to the moments of our passage.

These are the people we see occasionally—we know them by name, what is momentarily on their mind, perhaps what they do for a living… and that's just about all. They may be neighbors, co-workers, or one of the grocery store clerks where we like to shop. Basically we know *who* they are, but there isn't much depth to the relationship. Our knowledge of them is fuzzy around the edges—never really in focus.

This, of course, is the level where all relationships must begin, and can eventually become the foundation for a deeper friendship. But we must understand that most of our relationships in life will be no more than "friends along the way."

And that's okay. That's as it should be. Just as a photographer cannot focus on every item he sees through his lens, neither can we focus our attention on every individual who happens to cross our path. To begin with, we simply don't have *time*. Nor would such an effort be productive. It would be humanly impossible to treat every acquaintance as we would a regular companion or intimate friend.

This, then, is the first sort of relationship which God provides. And like those that follow, it is a "good" part of a creation God declared good. Like the sunshine that splashes across our path, the cool breeze that invigorates us, and the flowers that nod in the wind as we make our way from here to there, these casual friends bring delight and enrichment to our days.

## Companions—*"Friends for the hike"*

The next level of relationship speaks of friends who choose to be together for a time and enjoy something together.

You don't simply pass these people on the path, you've chosen to accompany each other for awhile. To walk in the same direction. There is common interest and common activity. This would be like an individual who says to you, "You like to hike the wilderness trails, and I like to hike the wilderness trails. Let's plan a trip together this October to see the leaves in the northern Cascade mountains."

So you hike the mountain trails, take rolls of pictures, and experience something happy and engaging together. Yet you might not see one another again for some time—when the pictures are developed!

Those who share this level of friendship appreciate many common activities and pursuits: They golf, they swim, they do aerobics three times a week, they quilt, they take painting classes, they study books in the Bible, they prowl antique shops, or they just relax over iced tea on the back deck and enjoy long conversations. They have a common interest and find delight in doing it together. They plan a time to go, enjoy the ride there together, and stop for coffee on the way home. It is good companionship.

These are the friends we spend more time with. They may be a friend from work or church, a neighbor who likes to chat on a regular basis, or just someone who shares a hobby. These friends come in all shapes and forms, but they do not come in the abundance of those casual acquaintances we meet "along the way." We can only maintain so many of these "friends for the hike" sort of relationships—and each of us has our own limit based on time, energy, and other commitments.

With these friends, we not only know *who* they are, but *what* they're about. We know their interests—what excites them and what bores them. We know what they plan to do in the future as well as where they've been in the past. We know not only *who*, but *what*.

These friends bring us a wealth of new insights from their perspectives on the world. In fact, they open up new worlds—worlds of knowledge or experience that may have been completely foreign to us.

What would life be without such compatible companions? Our favorite activities have twice the delight when we experience them along with someone else.

And that is precisely the way our wise Creator designed it to be.

## Intimate Friends—*"Friends for the journey"*

These are friends who don't simply accompany one another on a hike; they sit by the alpine lake together. They have chosen to draw apart and cherish the time together. They love sharing the distant view, the beauty of the flowers, and the sparkling water. But most of all, they value sharing their hearts with one another. They find that in the matters most important to their hearts, they see things through the same lens. They vibrate to the same note. They are bonded to one another.

These are the people we know on a deeper level—we know not only *who* they are and *what* they do, but we also know *why* they are and *where* they are.

These are neither casual acquaintances nor sometime companions. They are friends for the journey—the long haul. Lifetime friends.

When we experience this type of close friendship, we enter into a relationship of commitment and intimate sharing. But this level of friendship doesn't "just happen." Sometimes it may *seem* that way— there are those special times when we just *click* with another person and feel like we've known them all of our lives. But in reality even these close friendships require careful care and maintenance. Like any treasure they will grow more precious with time—if they are carefully tended and cherished.

> *Friendship is the greatest of worldly goods.*
> C. S. Lewis

> *Make new friends*
> *And keep the old*
> *One is silver*
> *The other's gold.*

---

See illustrated chart of the three levels of relationships on page 90.

# Understanding an Intimate Friendship

What are the ingredients of a truly significant relationship? What makes a deep friendship "deep"? What do we look for in such a friendship…and how do we know when we find it?

## – *Mutual attraction*

It probably all begins right here. There are some people we just plain like. Right off the top. Right from the start. There are things about this individual that appeal from our first meeting—her sense of humor…his quiet thoughtfulness…her warm sincerity.

In other words, you respond emotionally to this person. Without such mutual attraction, there is no momentum towards depth.

## – *Emotional openness*

Some of us have problems developing deep relationships because we tend to be emotionally closed. We are out of touch with our feelings or we don't know how to express them. Positive emotions are acceptable perhaps, but not negative ones—or vice versa.

If we do not experience and appropriately express all kinds of feelings, we don't "connect" with others deeply. We are distant emotionally even though we may outwardly project warmth.

Fear of rejection and lack of trust can hold us back. Making deep relationships is scary. We will be rejected by some. Not all are trustworthy. Refusing to risk and remaining emotionally distant may be a relief and seem safe, but…there is a terrific cost. We have no one to have deep fellowship with, to know us, to meet some of our deep needs. No intimate friends.

## — *Shared responsibility*

Good friendships may generate spontaneously, but they require effort to keep the momentum alive. Participants in an intimate friendship will not shy away from the mutual responsibility required to keep the relationship on track and growing. No friendship will ever survive long-term when only one person takes the responsibility to feed and cultivate it. If the other person neglects to invest time and effort to maintain the relationship, it telegraphs a signal which reads, *I really don't care that much.* Inevitably, the one doing all the work feels devalued— and may become too discouraged to maintain the effort.

## — *Like beliefs*

Intimate friends share similar beliefs. Like values means there's general agreement and compatibility over such things as the use of time and money, the choice of activities, and above all, moral values. That's one reason why a marriage between one who personally knows the Lord

and one who doesn't will face serious built-in problems. Their oppos-
ing value systems make conflict almost inevitable.

### — *Similar interests*

These closest-of-friendships thrive on a variety of shared activities and
interest areas. No, that doesn't mean that every interest has to be the
same. *Some* variety is desirable—and offers opportunity for discovery
and growth. Nevertheless, the relationship needs a solid base of mutual
"likes," and each friend needs to demonstrate genuine enthusiasm for
the enthusiasms of the other.

### — *Common goals*

It's difficult to maintain intimacy if our goals are pushing us in diverging
directions. If we're not intending to walk along the same path as our
friend, there will be little chance for depth in the relationship. Our
hearts aren't at the same place…and the natural tendency will be to
drift apart.

### — *Having fun!*

An important element of the intimate relationship is that we relish the
same kinds of things as our friend. We can be comfortable alone with
our friend, or within a social setting. Their form of humor and
communication doesn't embarrass us. Some friends seem to get along

well in private, but fall apart in groups—or vice versa. If we enjoy the same kinds of activities and people, our friendship will grow richer and stronger.

## Allow Space

Intimate friends respect each other's need for separateness as well as togetherness. They are not so desperate to overcome their feelings of loneliness or "not belonging" that they struggle to maintain a suffocating closeness. Instead, they will allow for mystery in the other. It is this that attracts us to each other, and entices us with the anticipation of "more to be discovered" a little farther down the trail.

> *Relationships are like dances in which people try to find whatever happens to be the mutual rhythm in their lives.*
> Fred Rogers

## Time and Focused Effort

Intimate friendships cannot be hurried; they need to age and season with the passing weeks, months, and years. We human beings are complex creatures. It takes time to discover a person's *true* values— not just those to which they give mental assent.

It also takes a focused effort to discover another's aims in life and what lies behind his or her lifestyle. We need to discover whether we have basic *alikeness* in these areas. Without those solid foundations, we will never experience the "oneness" needed for a deep relationship. Often this means rolling up your sleeves and plunging into your friend's fondest interest areas. If you're already close in other areas, you'll most likely find yourself having a good time…and enhancing the foundation of your friendship.

## The Trust Factor

The *most* important thing our heart wants to know about any friend is this: Can I trust you?

Can we trust our friends with our secrets and confidences? With our hopes and dreams? With our weaknesses and failures? Will they laugh at us, look down on us, or reject us if we do? Can we trust them not to use such privileged information against us someday?

How we long for intimate friends we can really trust! And how wealthy we are when we find them!

## Stand by Your Friend

There is still something more needed for an intimate-friend relationship…and it may be the most important element of all. That "something" is commitment—such a rare quality these days!

Some may say, "I make deep short-term relationships." Really? I wonder. The depth of sharing in such brief friendships may give an adrenaline rush that satisfies…for the time. But what is left when it's over? What is the aftertaste? Emptiness again. There is a danger of becoming adrenaline junkies in these so-called friendships.

So often, we want the pleasures of deep relationships without the responsibilities. Recently I noticed a difference in the commitment level in such a small thing as the way I sign personal letters. Mine end with a simple "Love, Pam."

My grandmother Pamela, however, born in the 1800's, signed her letters "Your devoted friend, Mela." In today's vocabulary the word "Love" has become an expression of warmth and feeling (but often with no strings attached). "Devoted friend" adds that commitment of will.

Commitment involves sticking around when our friend seems preoccupied and distracted, experiences deep difficulty, or endures the humiliation of failure. It means hanging in there when we haven't been getting what we want out of the relationship. It means staying with it when the well of spontaneous affection seems nearly dry. It is a commitment to our friend's highest good—regardless of personal cost.

*Love is patient and kind.*
*Love trusts all things,*
*Believes all things.*
*Endures all things…*
I Corinthians 13

# What It Takes to Be a Friend

Cultivating an intimate relationship involves these three things: really knowing a person, developing trust, and loving him unconditionally.

## What's to Know?

As individuals, we need to be people with interests, established values, and goals in life. Without these we have little to share. We can't expect good relationships to develop just because we are alive and human. Friendships don't exist in a vacuum. They grow out of the turf of our shared enjoyments, convictions, and achievements.

*People who simply want friends can never make any.*
*The very condition of having Friends is that we should want some-*
*thing else besides Friends....Friendship must be about something,*
*even if it were only an enthusiasm for dominoes or white mice.*
*Those who have nothing can share nothing; those who*
*are going nowhere can have no fellow-travelers.*
C. S. Lewis

## Open Your Heart Door

Before someone else can come to know me—really know me—I need to learn how to share myself intimately and appropriately. I don't share deeply with everyone, only those with whom I have a continuing and close relationship.

There are those who unload their life stories, their "uglies," and all their fondest dreams in about the first minute and a half after meeting someone. As has been said, "They don't make friends, they take hostages!"

All instant intimacy is an oxymoron. It is a substitute for the real thing. And when it withers and fades (as it inevitably must, having no roots), it leaves those involved feeling dissatisfied and puzzled as to "what went wrong."

For true depth I must carefully share myself at about the same level of self-disclosure as my friend is sharing. I move into more intimate sharing s-l-o-w-l-y, by letting my friend know what I am thinking and feeling. I speak about my convictions and tell my joys and disappointments. I let her know my dreams. I open up regarding my weaknesses, failures, and fears as well as my victories and successes. *I let myself be known.*

Without self-disclosure I can have numbers of good friends, but no intimate ones. If I am going to have the help, support, encouragement, and reproof I need from my friend, I must be open with her. One of the greatest benefits of openness is that as she accepts me just as I am, really knowing me, I experience the kind of unconditional love God has for me.

> *When two people love each other deeply*
> *and are committed for life,*
> *they have usually developed*
> *a great volume of understandings*
> *between them.*
> *They share countless private memories*
> *unknown to the rest of the world.*
> Dr. James Dobson
> *Love for a Lifetime*

## Know Your Friend

Listening—really listening—to another individual is not as easy as it might seem. Yet intimate friendship cannot blossom apart from such listening. Whole-hearted listening. Careful listening. Intense listening. I listen not to analyze her but to truly understand her. Oh, how our hearts long for someone to care about the way we feel! And after I've listened I need to respond.

Too often, however, the scenario reads something like this: My friend has something on her mind, something extremely important to her. She comes to me and tells me all about it. I hear her out, but as soon as she finishes (or pauses to gather her thoughts), I start on something about myself. It may be something similar that I have experienced or something on my mind. I have "listened," but there was no *response* on my part, no real entering into her problem.

When you really listen to a friend, you hear her. You track with the conversation. You give eye contact, deliberately closing out distractions. You become *involved* in what she is talking about. You ask appropriate questions. You encourage her to keep on talking until she has thoroughly talked the subject through. You endeavor to respond not only to the content of what she said, but also to the emotions behind her words—her anger, her joy, her sorrow, her anxiety.

> *He who loves understands,*
> *and he who understands loves.*
> *One who feels understood feels loved,*
> *and one who feels loved feels sure*
> *of being understood.*
> Paul Tournier
> *To Understand Each Other*

Sometimes we fool ourselves into thinking that we listen when we allow another to speak. *I keep quiet for two minutes while she talks and then I get my turn.* Sometimes we hardly wait for the other person to finish (or take a breath) so we can speak.

But that isn't listening.

How can we respond to what the other person says or doesn't say if we haven't really listened? How do we know where she is really coming from? When we fail to listen and respond, we miss out on becoming genuinely involved with her—both mentally and emotionally.

If I am going to develop and maintain a good friendship, I must be able to both reveal who I am and to listen to the other person. Most of us are stronger in one area than the other. One will come more naturally. It takes real work to correct the weakness. But without a good balance of both elements, the relationship will become lopsided, and someone will eventually feel slighted.

## Can We Talk?

Another area that requires hard work is that of *confrontational skills.* When we disagree with a friend, what method do we use to work things out? What method does she use? Do our methods work?

There are three common ways of dealing with conflict, yet only one of them will really accomplish anything worthwhile.

We can *strike out, walk out,* or *talk out.*

*Striking out* can be done directly with angry words, or obliquely with sarcasm. It can even be conveyed through voice tone. When we strike out at a loved one we can wound the relationship and destroy the potential for growth.

*Walking out* can be accomplished by physically leaving, emotionally withdrawing, or clamming up. When we walk out, we send a hurtful message—we show our friend that she is not worth the time or effort that it takes to work through the problem. This puts us in the position of power and control.

Many of us know of no other way of handling conflict apart from these two. *Talking out* is foreign to us, and requires a higher level of concentration and practice. It means allowing the other person to have his full say and really listening to his point of view and emotional response concerning the problem at hand. It means stating your point of view and emotional repsonse without cutting him down or threatening him with reprisal. It means working hard to come to an agreement that will be satisfactory—though perhaps not the first choice of both parties.

When we can't come to an agreement, it means concentrating on the areas where we *do* agree, building the continuing relationship around that base.

Many, many years ago, a wise pastor said to me, "When you find yourself disagreeing with someone, take your eyes off the 95 percent where you don't agree and keep them focused on the 5 percent where you do."

That has turned out to be one of the most helpful pieces of advice I've ever received.

## Can I Trust You with My Heart?

An intimate friend is someone we can depend on to remain loyal and keep confidences. She is like a safe harbor, a person we can turn to for protection and shelter. But she is also like a beacon of light, whom we can count on to uphold the truth in love...even when it isn't easy. She is someone who won't turn my words against me, or use my confidences to hurt me. And the greater the friendship—the greater the trust level needed!

The flip side of this kind of loyalty and trust is that I will never betray my friend, nor will I desert her. I will be supportive of her in all her interests, endeavors, and heartaches. I will be loyal to her and defend her when she is being spoken against by others.

*Love one another deeply from the heart.*
1 Peter 1:22

## More Precious than Gold

Trustworthiness is a rare jewel. It is noteworthy that the first thing said about God's ideal woman in Proverbs 31 is:

*The heart of her husband trusts in her,*
*And he will have no lack of gain.*
*She does him good and not evil*
*All the days of her life.*
Proverbs 31:11-12, NASB

How much it means to have a supportive person alongside of you! How many friendships and marriages fail for lack of such support!

What does it mean to "do good" to another? It means I will do all within my power to improve my friend's life, to add to her sense of worth, to help her develop her potential to the fullest, to "encourage her to love and good works." I am not in the friendship to compete with her, but to help her do the work and will of God.

What does it mean not to "do evil"? It means I will defend her. I will not betray her. I will not give others ammunition to use against her, nor will I talk behind her back, tell of her faults, or injure her reputation. I will be honest with her and honor my promises.

## More Loyal than a Brother

I will not desert my friend. And this means so much more than just leaving physically. It also means *I will not withdraw my acceptance.* I will not make that acceptance conditional upon her complying with me or cooperating with me or conforming to my standards.

It means I will neither withdraw my interest nor my care. Temptations to desert may arise when others come along who seem to have "more to offer." Loyalty means I will steadfastly refuse that option.

In his book, *To Understand Each Other*, Paul Tournier speaks of three stages in the marital relationship. The first is the "honeymoon stage," marked by a sense of spontaneous mutual understanding.

In the second stage, Tournier points out that faults—often very serious faults—are found, and with them the well-known expression: "I can't understand him!"

The third stage, he says, can go one of two ways. The first of these takes the form of endless disputing—or the capitulation of one who gives up his own personality for the sake of "peace," or both withdraw from each other and create separate lives becoming more and more secretive.

The second way is accepting the reality of the partner as he is and making a real attempt to understand him. Since he does not feel capable of overcoming his faults and, therefore, strongly reacts to criticism, "he can be helped in quite a different fashion: simply by loving him, not so much for his qualities as for his problems. He can be helped by simply understanding him, understanding what he missed in his childhood years and what is still missing, and by seeking to fill that need."[1]

---

1   *To Understand Each Other*, Paul Tournier, pp. 32-33, 1966, Westminster/ John Knox.

While these three stages can be most clearly seen in the marital relationship, any truly intimate friendship may experience much of the same progression. Loyalty means that at no stage do I withdraw my acceptance. I give myself to understanding and helping my friend.

When a spouse or a friend knows that I will do him good and not evil and that I will continue on that course all the days of my life, his heart can trust; it can be safe and at rest in me.

"All the days of my life" speaks of the commitment of an intimate friend. My grandmother once said to me, "An intimate friend is the most valuable possession you will ever have—and the most costly."

Commitment *costs*. There is much giving, much self-sacrifice involved. These are not trendy words in today's culture. And the truth is, they never have been easy. If, however, I want to develop and maintain close, rich friendships, this is the path I must be willing to follow.

## With My Whole Heart

Relationships involve not only knowing another and developing trust, but the emotional component of loving. Our hearts as well as our heads must be satisfied. Giving and receiving love is as much a human need as food and water. Without love our souls become parched and famished.

What does the love of a truly good friend feel like? It feels warm! That warmth needs to be consistent—not warm one day and cool the next. Personal warmth is the most powerful way we have of saying "I like you." It is the strongest factor in making and maintaining relationships. I need to convey warmth to my friend—that I like her, approve her, and accept her as she is.

*Affection needs to be verbalized.* Too often after relationships have developed to a certain stage, we settle into a satisfied silence, taking for granted the other person knows how we feel. And as much as we all enjoy the comfort of familiar relationships, we still need to provide and receive continual reassurance. Sometimes it's through words, sometimes it's more....

*Ways to show I care…*
*A note or card*
*Share a favorite book*
*An unexpected phone call*
*Flowers*
*A homecooked meal*
*A moonlit walk*
*Antique shopping together*
*A cup of good coffee or tea*
*An unexpected favor*
*A follow-up on the problems*
*she shared*

## Ask Forgiveness

Relationships thrive and bloom in the soil of forgiveness.

Since we are all fallen people—though we bear the image of God—we need to forgive and be forgiven. Often. Over and over. The Bible puts it directly:

*Bear with each other and forgive whatever grievances you may*
*have against one another. Forgive as the Lord forgave you.*
*And over all these virtues put on love.*
Colossians 3:13-14

*Forgiveness is like the violet*
*Sending forth its pure fragrance*
*On the heel of the boot*
*Of the one who crushed it.*
Source Unknown

Forgiveness comes in many forms. Sometimes we simply learn to bear with another's weaknesses and idiosyncrasies. And we forgive silently. At other times, we seek to clear the air immediately, dealing with misunderstandings as soon as they arise.

The true basis for forgiving my friend lies in the all-important knowledge that I am a forgiven person. I can forgive—I *must forgive—because* God has forgiven me in Christ. When it is "my turn" to extend forgiveness, then, I need to freely and graciously grant it to my friend—with no strings attached—and move on. If we allow grievances to stockpile without resolving them, the relationship will eventually buckle under the load, sustaining serious damage.

The Bible makes it crystal clear. "If your brother sins against you, go and show him his fault, just between the two of you" (Matthew 18:15). Stony or icy silence is a power-and-control technique, and is not of God. On the other hand, "if you are offering your gift at the altar and there remember that your brother has something against you, leave your gift there. First go and be reconciled to your brother; then come and offer your gift." (Matthew 5:24).

The first move is always yours!

## Remembering to Love Those We Love

There was a framed poem on my grandmother's dresser that made a deep impression on me as a child. So much so that I memorized it. I owe much to the author. Part of the poem reads like this:

> *They say the world is round and yet,*
> *I often think it's square,*
> *So many little hurts we get*
> *From corners here and there.*
> *But there's one great truth in life I've found,*
> *While journeying to the West*
> *The only folks we really wound*
> *Are those we love the best.*
>
> *The choicest garb, the sweetest grace,*
> *Are oft to strangers shown;*
> *The careless mien, the frowning face,*
> *Are given to our own.*
> *We flatter those we scarcely know,*
> *We please the fleeting guest,*

*And deal full many a thoughtless blow*
*To those who love us best.*
Ella Wheeler Wilcox


*Dear children, let us not love with words or tongue but with actions*
*and in truth. This then is how we know that we belong to the truth.*
1 John 3:18-19

# Good Relationships Need Structure

Good relationships require both good people and good structure.

But we don't like to hear that word "structure" in relation to friendships, do we? It sounds just a little "clinical." It grates on the ear a bit. We feel friendships should be...spontaneous. Free. Relaxed.

Yet lack of definition is precisely the reason why so many relationships fade and fail. Every relationship that you are in right now, every relationship that you will ever be in will be structured. And the truth is, if you don't play a part in establishing that structure, you may not like the framework that eventually takes shape—and you'll begin to withdraw from the relationship physically or emotionally.

## "Friends Along the Way"...or More?

We need to accept just how much we do and don't have to give in any given relationship. To do this we learn to structure the limits. How much time are you each going to put into this relationship? How much time can be counted on?

I think of a neighbor of mine. The way our relationship is structured, she feels free to come over for about a half hour on Saturday mornings. I feel free to do the same. We don't expect to spend three hours together on Saturday. We understand the depth of our relationship.

What will be the limits of involvement? In times of crisis, we must do what we can to help others—regardless of our level of friendship. But there are limits to involvement even then. The good Samaritan paid for but did not personally care for the wounded man at the inn. On a day-to-day basis, limits of involvement must be structured. Without such limits we are robbed of time and energy to meet our responsibilities to ourselves and others.

*Each man should give what he has decided in his heart to give,*
*not reluctantly or under compulsion, for God loves a cheerful giver.*
2 Corinthians 9:7

While this scripture refers to financial giving, I believe it states the basis of all true giving. In friendships we give more than money, we give ourselves. We need to decide before the Lord "how much" and "to whom." There is only so much of us to give!

## Structure the Responsibilities

What responsibilities will you or won't you take on? In the course of friendship, we often help each other out. Yet if we are going to keep from presuming on one another, that "friendly assistance" also requires some structure.

"Since you're working, I'll take your daughter with mine to school and home each day; but you'll need to make other arrangements for her sports, appointments, and other activities."

What responsibilities can your friend expect you to assume? If you are asked to do something beyond what you really want to do, then *say so*. Graciously, kindly, firmly. Yes, it's difficult! But it is the kindest thing to do. It's foolish to accept an unwanted responsibility that will leave you with clenched teeth, upset stomach, and a resentful spirit. That sort of "willingness" is really unfair to your friend—and can only harm a relationship.

## Structure the Expectations

What are the expectations? Determining this may require some careful "think-time." We often find ourselves uncomfortable with the structure of certain relationships, but we're reluctant to say anything negative— or it's difficult to declare what we are comfortable with.

Too often, we "promise the world" as we enter into a relationship. "Any time you need me just say so." Taking me at my word, my friend may request much more than I intend to give. I want to back out of it. I make some excuses. And then the other person really feels rejected. It's so easy to offer too much. It's important to establish realistic expectations from the beginning.

## Structure the Roles

Roles in a relationship also need definition: who I will be to you, and who you will be to me. "No, I won't be your mother. No, I cannot be your sister. No, I won't be your child. No, I cannot be your best friend."

It's vital to clarify roles early on. If you don't give any input, a role will be established for you. You may not like that role. You may be upset and feel trapped. As a result, the friendship you offer will be tentative and reluctant, leaving the other person hurt and confused. How much better to make it known right from the beginning what you will be. Then the other person knows where he stands. He has the opportunity to decide if he wants the kind of friendship you have to offer.

Structure, then, isn't some intrusive, confining box we impose upon a relationship. It is the trellis that supports our friendships and allows them to climb to their natural height…and bloom.

# Avoiding the Snags in Relationships

FRAGILE

**FRAGILE**

The overarching problem in relationships is expecting others to fill a void in our hearts that only God can fill.

No friend, spouse, group, or gathering can meet our deepest longings for unconditional love, belongingness, and wholeness. Not realizing or admitting this, we can place impossible burdens on each other to take away our loneliness. Yet ironically, when we make such demands, we call out the other person's sense of inadequacy and he *retreats* rather than moving towards us.

We live with the expectation that mutual openness and togetherness will solve our problems. Yet only God's unconditional love can dispel our isolation, and it is our unity with Him alone that gives the belongingness and wholeness our hearts crave.

> *You belong to Christ; and Christ belongs to God.*
> 1 Corinthians 3:23, NASB

Nevertheless, the haunting pain of loneliness has the capacity to overcome our perspective and good sense. In our desperation, we might find ourselves rushing in where we ought to tread lightly. The most common problem in relationships, therefore, is that of moving into depth too quickly.

"A righteous man," wrote Solomon, "is cautious in friendship" (Proverbs 12:26).

In other words, he proceeds slowly. He doesn't overcommit himself. Making friends with care and thoughtfulness is basic to good and lasting relationships.

## Through Summer and Winter

I remember as a little girl I would sometimes run home from school with big news to share with my grandmother.

"Oh Nanna! I have met the most wonderful little girl! We're going to be real pals. She just moved here and she's in my class, and oh, she's tremendous! We're going to be best friends."

My grandmother would say to me, "Dear, you have to summer with her and winter with her, and summer with her again. Then tell me."

There's great wisdom in that. It means you really get to know a person before entering into the commitments that an intimate friendship requires.

## The Control Trap

Another common problem in friendships develops when one person tries to control the other. The deeper the friendship grows, the more vulnerable we become at any level. But the intimate relationship in particular provides fertile ground for the stronger personality to control the one who yields more easily. This type of manipulation can occur on both conscious and subconscious levels. Yet whatever form that control may take, it's poison in a relationship. It may be quick poison or it may be slow poison, but it will always weaken and often kill a friendship.

The word *friend* comes from the Old English root word *freon*—meaning "to love," akin to *freo*—meaning "free."

I must leave the other free—free to be herself. I must encourage her to have her own feelings...think her own thoughts...support her own causes...do things her own way...make her own decisions.

If I don't, she will feel she is being swallowed up and losing her own identity. Her alternatives are to either succumb to a destructive relationship or withdraw.

## Anything You Can Do, I Can Do Better

Competition is another toxic element that can taint a relationship. God's purpose for relationships is mutual help through cooperation.

But what happens when I want to be superior to my friend or spouse? I start to compete. Rivalry enters in. I want to look better, or perform better, or have more recognition. As a result, one of us has a sense of being threatened—and we may respond to such threats by attacking or withdrawing.

The relationship becomes strained or broken because somewhere along the line our objective shifts from "helping" to "winning."

*Let us not become conceited, provoking and envying each other.*
Galatians 5:26

## How Much Is Too Much?

Another common problem is that one person may desire a deeper level of relationship than the other. The minute this situation occurs, you have conflict. The person striving for the deeper level tends to "put on the pressure."

You may feel yourself being pushed into a level of relationship you don't want. And that makes you resistant. You feel invaded, closed in on. You pull away from your friend. It feels like that friend is always wanting to share, always wanting your time, always wanting to move into your territory. Give him one hour and he wants two. Rather than opening up, you find yourself looking for a back door.

## It Takes Two

What does this say to us, then? It says that you should never go any deeper in a relationship than the other person is ready to go. If you find yourself looking for an intimate "friend for the journey" sort of relationship, and yet sense your friend wants only a companionable "friend for the hike" relationship, you need to back up to where he or she is. The more you try to pressure for deeper sharing and a deeper commitment, the more you're going to push your friend away from you.

> *Seldom set foot in your neighbor's house—*
> *too much of you, and he will hate you.*
> Proverbs 25:17

This verse cautions us not to overstay our welcome. Better to create regret by leaving too early than by staying too long! But it also says if you push too hard on a relationship you will get resentment—not friendship.

## The Truth Can Hurt—at First

A number of years ago, I felt some very distinct pressure from a woman in my community. She was always giving me gifts. After a number of weeks, I felt I was being "bought." Obligated. And so I began to withdraw toward an acquaintance type of friendship. Really, I dreaded to see her come.

Finally I had the courage to say, "Look, this is what's happening. I'd like to have a good friendship with you. It may not be as deep as you'd like, but it could be a good friendship. There may not be intimate sharing, but we'll do things together that we both enjoy. Your gifts say to me that you're seeking a close friendship. And that makes me feel obligated. Frankly, the depth you seem to want isn't what I want right now. But I *would* like to have a friendship because I enjoy and appreciate you and want that to continue."

The woman was furious at me.

Well, I felt that was the end of that, but wished it hadn't ended that way. I tried to go on being kind, loving, and warm. But she was icy.

Within a few weeks, however, she came back to me and said, "You know, you're the first person who's had the courage to tell me what's wrong in my friendships. I've never had a friendship of any depth. People always back away from me and I never really knew what was wrong."

At first, it hurt her to know what was wrong. In time, however, she grasped a vital truth about relationships and how to gain and keep satisfying friendships.

## "I Only Need One Friend"

Having just one close friend can be another problem. This can lead to poverty of personality at best, and exclusiveness at the worst. Jealousy can easily slip into this "exclusive" sort of relationship. The friendship can fall into an unhealthy, even crippling pattern. Homosexual relationships, latent or overt, often stem from the "only one friend" category.

The "one friend" relationship is often a dependent relationship usually accompanied by possessiveness, hurt feelings, and jealousy. Any time a dependent relationship develops, the most loving thing you can do is to point out to your friend what is going on in the relationship *and refuse to allow yourself to be drawn into it or to respond to her demands or pleas.* This might seem "uncaring," and your friend may quickly try to heap guilt on your shoulders. But in fact, it is the truest expression of love in that circumstance. It refuses to further cripple your friend, and points the way back to a healthy relationship.

We need friendships at *all* levels. We should have many, many acquaintances. And we need many companionship friends. These friends bring a wealth of diversity into our lives. They have great treasures to give me, and hopefully I have some wealth to add to their lives as well. And then we need a special few whom we consider intimate friends.

My growth as a person will come in large measure through my friends. To limit that number to only one friend—for whatever reason—is to limit my growth.

## But There Is a Limit!

On the flip side of the one-close-friend danger, however, is the attempt to spread ourselves out with too many close friends. Solomon stated it well when he wrote:

> *A man of many companions may come to ruin,*
> *but there is a friend who sticks closer than a brother.*
> Proverbs 18:24

You and I are finite beings, and we need to understand and accept the fact that we have neither the time nor the emotional energy to maintain more than four or five really close friends. We must discipline ourselves to draw some limits…or "come to ruin" as Solomon expressed it.

When you examine the pattern of the Lord Jesus you find He had many acquaintances. He had the crowds—those who knew Him by name, perhaps followed Him from a distance, or even touched the hem of His cloak.

He also had nine disciples who were His companions, but not His most intimate friends. They spent a lot of time with Him and knew Him well, but they remained just slightly outside His innermost circle.

According to Scripture, Peter, James, and John were His most intimate friends. Mary, Martha, Lazarus, and Mary Magdalene were also in that special group.

Christ did not take all of His disciples to the Mount of Transfiguration.

Only Peter, James, and John. Nor did He ask everyone to watch with Him at Gethsemane. Only those three.

The Lord's pattern provides an ideal example for us. To try to maintain too many intimate relationships will leave us frustrated and our friends disappointed. In the meanwhile, we feel harried, pressured, and often guilty when we can't respond to those we feel committed to. We need to be as free as Christ was to draw limits.

## It Works Both Ways

We also need to allow our friend to be free and to accept his limits though we want a closer friendship.

The disciple Andrew has become one of my heroes. Consider the situation. He was one of John the Baptist's disciples. When John said "Behold, the Lamb of God," Andrew and an unnamed friend followed Jesus. They were His first followers.

When they asked the Lord where He was staying, He invited them to come with Him. They spent the rest of the afternoon and evening—perhaps the entire night—with Him. The next day Andrew brought his brother Peter to Jesus, saying he had found the Messiah. Andrew and Peter were fishing partners with James and John.

How difficult it must have been for Andrew to be the *one* of these four men who were close to each other—and yet not be chosen as one of the Lord's most intimate disciples. He wasn't one of "the three." He wasn't "in the loop" with Peter, James, and John. He wasn't privileged to see the Lord's glorification on the mountain. He had no opportunity to watch with Christ in the garden. But what a loyal friend and disciple he remained. It was he who brought the boy with the loaves and fishes to Jesus for the feeding of the five thousand. It was he, along with Philip, who brought the inquiring Greeks to Him—an event which prompted the Lord's sermon to the multitude concerning fruitfulness and His imminent death on the cross. It was here among the passover crowds that Andrew also heard the Father's voice from heaven answering His son.

Perhaps Andrew remembered John the Baptist's words when people told John that all were now going to Jesus instead of him. John had answered "a man can receive nothing unless it has been given him from heaven" (John 3:27).

You may desire a closer relationship than your friend really wants or God has given. But a "friend for the hike" relationship can be a rewarding, fulfilling, and ministering relationship. And if we try to force our way into a deeper level, or if we allow jealousy to creep in, it can spoil what God planned for our enjoyment and growth.

God knows very well how to bring good things into the lives of His much-loved children…in His own way and in His own time.

# Friendships with the Opposite Sex

Let me revisit that modern proverb I quoted earlier: "Involvement with people is always a very delicate thing...it requires real maturity to become involved and not get all messed up."

Never is this more true than in relationships between men and women.

After countless hours of counseling, teaching, and observing generations of young college men and women, I can speak with some seasoned assurance on this crucial, ever-volatile topic.

These friendships can be so very enriching and highly rewarding that certainly they need developing and nurturing. We stand in great need of what the opposite sex has to bring into our lives. Our view of relationships, of life, of meanings, is then seen with two sets of eyes, not one. We bring out qualities in one another that can otherwise lie dormant. We not only balance one another, we enhance one another. Just as the wise Creator intended.

The problem comes because of the fine line between companionship and intimate friendship. It arises because at the intimate level of friendship the attraction becomes incredibly strong. It is at this point that erotic love is easily aroused. While that can certainly happen at any level it is deeply fed at the intimate level.

If I can state anything with assurance, it is this: *Single men and women cannot maintain a deep and intimate relationship that is pure and healthy unless it is heading toward marriage.* To tell themselves anything else is patent foolishness. Eventually, someone is going to get hurt—perhaps profoundly. God made us sexual beings with sexual attraction. Deep intimacy of sharing between sexes arouses emotions and eventually desires for emotional or sexual fulfillment. Those desires generate a magnetic pull that cannot be adequately described—and must never be minimized.

*This is the way God designed us.* To try to maintain an intimate friendship with the opposite sex without an erotic component is going against nature. It is like telling the crocuses not to blossom in spring. This also holds true for married men and women who walk the danger-ous path of intimate opposite-sex relationships with someone other than their spouse.

## Undeclared Intentions

Careful navigation is also required in a dating relationship. To avoid misunderstanding, there is a very real need to keep declaring "where you are." It's so confusing and frustrating to a man or woman not to know where the other sees the relationship.

Let's assume, for example, that a man has been dating a woman for three or four months, and she doesn't know whether he's just enjoying a good friendship or is possibly working toward a lifetime commitment. It is most important for this man to declare where he is. If he doesn't take this step, she should ask him for some definition of their relationship.

He may say, "You know, I'm just looking for a friendship. I'm not thinking of a serious, on-going depth of relationship." Or, he may say, "You know, I really wonder whether or not this could be leading toward a very deep friendship and on to marriage."

## Mis-declared Intentions

Another problem arises when one *says* he or she simply wants a companion, but *acts* as an intimate friend would. If you say, "We're just friends, this isn't really heading to a lifetime commitment," then you must back away from intimate sharing. Non-intimate friends don't reveal secrets to one another.

Companions spend *maybe* an hour or two a week together. To indicate you would like to see the other many hours a week, and then to say "there's really nothing in this" is to send a very mixed message. The one receiving it needs to say, "We are friends, therefore we'll do the activities, we'll have the discussions that mild friends have and see each other occasionally." Otherwise one party can selfishly enjoy all the benefits of a relationship, the warmth and relief from loneliness, the satisfaction of the attention that feeds the ego—all without the accompanying commitment. One party luxuriates, while the other party feels cheated and is left with deep unsatisfied longings.

## Break-up of Dating Relationships

Having worked with college and post-college age couples for thirty-two years, I've developed some deep convictions about dating relationships. If a couple has been in a close relationship for a period of time, and for some reason one decides to break off the relationship, how should it be handled?

I am convinced there needs to be a clean, sharp break. The tendency is to take one step back to a companionship friendship so as "not to hurt" the other person. It seems a sensitive approach, but it simply doesn't work! The one whose heart is still involved, who still desires an intimate relationship, will consciously or unconsciously try to pull the other back to that deeper level.

Great amounts of energy and prayer can be concentrated on the hope of a change in the other party. The emotional focus of life remains centered on the one who is pulling away.

For the sake of the one still hurting, the one still emotionally involved, the relationship should be terminated. For the one breaking the relationship, it will mean the giving up of a good friendship. Painful as that is, it must be done for the good of the other. Until there is finality, his or her hopes, dreams, and expectations are kept alive. All the old responses are still there. Emotions are kept raw and can still produce deep pain a year, two years, or more later. There is no "kinder, gentler" gradual, step-by-step way to back out. A clean break is the most loving thing to do and represents a commitment to the friend's highest good.

Why? Because it gives that person time to grieve and to heal, so that eventually he or she can enter into deep involvement with another person. When both parties are happily involved with other committed dating relationships, then it may be possible for the original couple to have a companionship relationship, but not before.

Those who are ending a homosexual relationship likewise need to make a clean sharp break for health to be restored. Thinking that it is possible to drop back into a companionship relationship only leads to frustration, ongoing temptation, and almost always a return to the relationship and lifestyle.

## Is There Room for More?

The Lord's pattern is just as necessary for the married individual as for the single. Christian teaching places such a strong (and rightful) emphasis on the need for good communication and intimacy between husband and wife that we sometimes make it sound as though this is the only relationship needed.

Far from it! No spouse—not even Superman or Wonder Woman—can *possibly* meet all the emotional needs of the other for understanding and intimacy. We can drive one another away with excessive expectations and demands. Too heavy a burden is placed on the marriage. The marriage will be much richer and healthier if the spouses separately and together have many other relationships at varying levels—bearing in mind that intimate relationships are reserved for our spouse and members of our own sex.

## Caution—Danger Zone Ahead

Let's come back to the "red flag" areas of opposite sex relationships. Deep sharing between the sexes—outside the God-given provision of marriage—is an area of great hazard…and potential tragedy.

It doesn't matter if the attraction begins at the office, over the back fence, or in a church pew. For the married person what starts as a healthy companionship with someone of the opposite sex (let's say with a co-worker) can slide imperceptibly into the intimate level, and a husband or wife finds he or she is emotionally involved with someone outside the marriage. While physical adultery may not occur, emotional, psychological adultery—which is really deeper—does. The spouse has been displaced at the center of the heart. The spouse has been de-frauded, the covenant of love broken.

It is exceedingly easy to rationalize extramarital relationships, whether physical or psychological. The latter is certainly the easiest. "Since I am not allowing myself intercourse I am being true to my vows." The person thinking this can see himself or herself as God's appointed rescuer, or as a needed father or mother figure, or as a spiritual companion or director.

On the other hand, they may see this intimate friend as one God has brought into their life to awaken them to deeper emotions, a deeper knowledge of God, and a deeper and expanded personal growth. When the relationship is seen in a spiritual context or as a spiritual bond, it is most difficult to acknowledge the truth and to take corrective action.

The mind can always justify what the heart wants. "Why turn my back on the life-giving joy that God has blessed me with? Those that question our relationship just don't understand God's ultimate purposes for Christian men and women." Yes, the deception is great and it often takes a direct working of God to reveal it and bring those involved to repentance.

Once it is realized that the emotional line has been crossed there needs to be a clean, sharp break in the relationship level, responding to the other only as civility requires. Emotions are too near the surface, memories too pleasant, desires too strong.

Certainly only the grace of God and His moment by moment enablement can cause us to make and maintain this break. He promises to be there for us always.

*For we do not have a high priest who is unable to sympathize with our weaknesses, but we have one who has been tempted in every*

*way, just as we are—yet was without sin.  Let us then approach the throne of grace with confidence, so that we may receive mercy and find grace to help us in our time of need.*
Hebrews 4:15-16

# The Bond of Commitment

Any intimate relationship, if it's ever going to deepen, requires a strong, far-reaching commitment. This is equally true in man-to-man, or woman-to-woman friendships. (Marriage, of course, is built upon *total* commitment. Nothing less will do.)

Commitment is the bond that keeps relationships intact through every storm that rolls over the horizon. There will be times when your friend isn't free to do what you want to do. Friends may marry before you do, and naturally begin to invest time and energy in their new home and family. They may find themselves with not much time to invest in the friendship.

What do you do then? Drop them?

Not if you've made a commitment! You weather through that time. *Do not forsake your own friend or your father's friend...*(Proverbs 27:10 NASB).

Friends may become preoccupied with new interests or wrestle with heavy, emotionally-draining problems. They may not be functioning well physically. They may not be warm and responsive. Is that the time to abandon the friendship?

Not if you've made a commitment! Your friend may need you more than ever before.

*A friend loves at all times,*
*and a brother is born for adversity.*
Proverbs 17:17

Why are you in the friendship to begin with? For what you can receive? For what you can get out of it to meet your own needs and stroke your own ego? No, following the example of our Lord, we enter into relationships to give and to bless. There are seasons in every relationship where one is called on to give disproportionately to the other. There may be years with a difficult elderly parent or a lifetime with an indifferent spouse. Here is where commitment is tested, and here is where you will encounter God's greatest blessings.

## The Ultimate Commitment

What does the Lord say about the way friendships should operate? *Lay down your life for your friends* (John 15:13).

He laid down His life for those who deserted Him in the garden, who scattered from Him in the crisis, and who betrayed Him in the palace. He laid down His life for the disloyal and the disinterested. And it is this laid-down life, He tells us, that leads us along the way of joy and fruitfulness.

When in self-interest I ask, "What's in this for me?" He would restore me to His purpose for relationships and have me ask, "What can I give?"

There is only one way to be this true friend. Human love will always fail. The demands are too great. Self love is too strong. Only as I consistently and habitually depend on the Lord to pour His love out through me can I do what He commands—to love as He has loved me. His is a sacrificial, self-giving love. I am completely devoid of that kind of love—only the Holy Spirit can produce this quality in me.

> *My commandment is this: Love each other as I have loved you.*
> John 15:12

## The Friend Above All

Meanwhile, I have a Friend who never changes. One who meets the deepest heart need. That is His commitment to me.

But what of my commitment to Him? At which "level" do I place my relationship with this One who has loved me unconditionally? From the Lord's questions to Peter when He asked, "Do you love me?" after His resurrection, it is clear that He longs for the deepest love relationship.

Are we "friends for the journey"—lifelong companions? Do I look forward to those times together when I can truly share all my thoughts and feelings with Him, knowing I'll be understood and accepted and loved? Do I arrange my schedule to make those times alone with Him when He shares the interests and goals of His heart with me? Does my heart yearn for an ever-deepening intimacy with Him? Are our times alone the greatest joy of my life, the one thing I can't and won't do without?

If we haven't yet attained that level of relationship…are we "friends for the hike"? Are there appointed times—now and then—when we meet and share activities and enjoy one another's companionship? I may not do much listening in our walk together, but I tell Him about the things that concern me and ask for His help. When we haven't been together for awhile, I find myself missing His company.

Perhaps, after all, we are more like "friends along the way." My encounters with Him tend to be unplanned, haphazard. They're wonderful when they occur—they brighten my days and warm my nights—but we really don't spend much time together. I am left not really knowing Him too well.

What sort of friend does He find *me* to be? Am I involved in His interests and goals? Are my values like His? Am I a trustworthy friend— one who won't betray or desert? How deep is my love, my commitment? How much love do I express toward Him?

In the book of Hosea, the Lord's heart mourns over the fickle love of His people. He says: "What can I do with you, Ephraim? What can I do with you, Judah? Your love is like the morning mist, like the early dew that disappears" (Hosea 6:4).

If I want to deepen my relationship with the Lord, I must go about it as I would with an earthly friend. In other words, I must seek Him out. Open my life to Him. Rearrange my day for time to be alone with Him. Make His interests, His values the plumb line for my life. And as I do, I find to my astonishment that He has been seeking me with an even far greater intensity.

## His Commitment to Me

No matter how committed and loving a relationship I have with any others, no one but God can meet my deepest longings. No one else can turn my loneliness into fulfillment. He and He alone can transform the sense of isolation into togetherness, because He has joined me to Himself forever.

As for His commitment, He will never break His covenant of love, His vows to me. His love initiated our relationship and maintains it. He is infinitely interested in all that concerns me. His Spirit draws me out and lifts me up.

The One who controls the universe is devoted to me. It is a devotion that springs out of love, not duty. He is always devoted to my highest good.

Of all the qualities I want in a human friend, loyalty stands at the top of the list. I find that quality, to the ultimate degree, in the Lord. He promises a "loyal love," and that He will never betray or abandon me. He will never replace me in His heart because someone more attractive to Him has come along. He will neither forget nor desert me "all my days."

*Heav'n and earth may fade and flee,*
*First-born light in gloom decline;*
*But while God and I shall be,*
*I am His and He is mine.*[1]

My heart longs to be known, to be understood. I yearn for someone who knows me deeply, accepts me, and delights in me. The Lord knows all my problems. He feels every bump in my daily road. He hears my every sigh in the night. He knows my particular temptations, my failures, and how hard I've tried. He knows and celebrates my smallest victories—some so little I would be embarrassed to mention them to anyone else.

He knows me through and through and through. My uglies. My lack of love. My selfish indulgences. My stubborn pride. Yet instead of turning from me He looks at me with eyes of deepest love and tenderness. As He brings these areas to my attention, He reminds me afresh that He lives within me every minute of the day, conforming me to His image.

How often I have to ask His forgiveness because my thoughts or acts spoil our fellowship. Yet His is no half-hearted forgiveness. He doesn't look at me with disgust or mere tolerance. He pardons freely and He holds no grudges. He *lavishes* His love on me.

1   *Loved With Everlasting Love*, George W. Robinson, 1890.

I am gripped by a thought I can scarcely grasp in return. It seems so utterly unbelievable. Yet it is eternally true…*God, the Creator and Ruler of the universe, chose me to be His child and to be His <u>friend</u>.*

*…I have called you friends…*
John 15:15, NASB

The Lord is a friend who nourishes and cherishes me. He enjoys me. He is consumed with the desire to bring forth the loveliness of Christ in me. He will prune, water, and feed me; He will plant me in the right environment to bear choice fruit for Him and for the refreshment of others.

As a faithful friend His strength and resources are there for me to call on. When my foes—whether outward or inward—are about to overwhelm me, He enfolds me with His strength. Oh, how our hearts yearn for this—someone to lean on, someone who will strongly support us.

His love holds steady through the days and months and years. As the hymnwriter puts it, "My love still ebbs and flows…no change Jehovah knows."

His love for me isn't "because" He saw something lovable in me. My love is always a reaction to something in the other person—something

I enjoy or something that meets my need. His love is pure action toward me—"uncaused," blazing love, continually reaching out to me.

He loved me when I was His enemy. His love is unconditional. I am not on trial with Him, nor will He ever place me on probation. His great desire is that I receive His love. It cannot be bought or earned. It is a gift.

He has proved His love for me. His was the ultimate of all giving, the greatest expression of love. He laid down His life for me on the cross to pay the penalty for my sins.

He has brought me into relationship with the heavenly Father, a relationship of love for all eternity.

Of all the relationships I might cultivate, cherish, and guard through the fleeting years, surely this friendship is worthy of my whole heart.

> *This is my beloved and this is my friend.*
> Song of Solomon 5:16, NASB

# Three Levels Chart

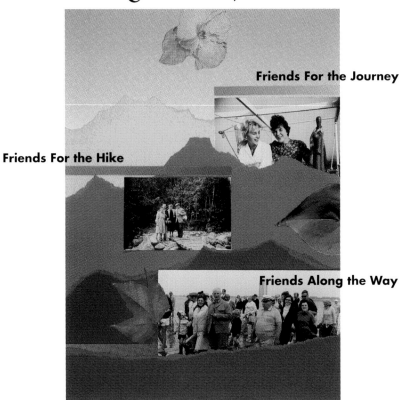

Friends For the Journey

Friends For the Hike

Friends Along the Way

Pamela Reeve enjoying His handiwork—the Alps

## About the Author...

For twenty-three years Dr. Pamela Reeve devoted her energies as Dean of Women at Multnomah Bible College in Portland, Oregon to counseling and leadership training. Her tenure at Multnomah, however, sharply contrasts with her early career goals.

After graduating with a degree in architecture from New York University, Pamela worked for seven years in the profession before realizing that the Lord was calling her to build people rather than structures. A move to California, teaching and administrative positions in a Christian high school, eight years public college teaching and counseling, and a graduate degree in education from UCLA followed. Today, she continues as a professor, counselor and advisor for Multnomah Biblical Seminary Women's Ministries programs.